SCHOOL OF BIBLICAL HERMENEUTICS

Keys for Correctly Interpreting God's Word

A ministry of:

Striving For Eternity Ministries

School of Biblical Hermeneutics
INTRODUCTION

Many Christians recognize that the Bible is the source of spiritual growth for their lives but become frustrated when they come to the text and attempt to gain an understanding of it. This study is designed to give the student of the Scriptures some of the keys to interpreting correctly the Word of God. Before we begin, it will benefit us to outline the objectives and the obstacles that will hinder your personal study.

I. The <u>Objectives</u>

   A. To help the student become more effective in interpreting the Word of God to the end that they may have a closer walk with Him and be ready to minister with the Word.

   B. To introduce the student to the various tools available for in-depth Bible study.

   C. To teach the student to use more effectively his/her English Bible.

   D. To assist the student in gaining a greater appreciation for the Word of God

II. The <u>Obstacles</u>

   A. No *Conversion*

   Spiritual things will have no bearing on the personal life of an unregenerated person (1 Corinthians 2:14).

   B. No *Commitment*

   Searching the deep things of God is a rewarding task, but it is work. A student must be committed to the study of the Word of God (2 Timothy 2:15)

   C. No *Church*

   A Bible-teaching church gives you opportunities not only to gain insight into passages, but to observe the process as well.

SECTION 1

An Appreciation of the Scriptures

The primary objectives of this kind of study focus on the methods of Bible study. In order to lay the foundations, however, it is essential to appreciate Scripture itself, no matter which text we are examining.

This section is indebted to John MacArthur and his book *How to Study the Bible*, Moody Press, 1982.

I. ATTRIBUTES OF THE BIBLE

    A. It is *Infallible.*

    Every word of the Bible is exactly how God had intended them to be (2 Timothy 3:16; Psalm 19:7)

    B. It is *Inerrant.*

    The Bible is without error. This focuses on the necessary relation between the *authenticity* of the words and the *authority* of its message.

    C. It is *Complete.*

    This truth is sometimes called *plenary*. This emphasizes the fact that nothing should be *added* to the Bible and nothing should be *subtracted* from it. (Revelation 22:18-19).

    D. It is *Authoritative.*

    The Bible is God's *self-revelation* of the One who has the right and power to command compliance in thought and deed upon His rational creatures.

    E. It is *Trustworthy.*

    All that God has said in His Word is sure and is either a present reality or will come to pass. This includes that statements of history, geography, and science are also trustworthy statements.

    F. It is *Eternal.*

    Heaven and earth will pass away before God's Word. The standards and precepts for character and morality will be in effect throughout eternity.

II. AUTHENTICITY OF THE BIBLE

It must be understood that we accept the authenticity of the Bible ultimately by faith. There are, however, certain realities that affirm the authenticity of the Bible.

A. Prophecy

Everything that the Bible has said would come to pass has come to pass.

"Peter Stoner, in his book *Science Speaks*, said that if you take just eight of the Old Testament prophecies Christ fulfilled (Stoner is a scientist in the area of mathematical probabilities), and add up the probabilities that these eight things could come to pass by accident, it would be one chance in 10^{17} that such an accident could happen – and yet every detail has come to pass. One chance in 10^{17} would be like filling the state of Texas with [sic] two-feet deep in silver dollars, putting an 'x' on one of them, and giving a blind man one pick. He'd have one chance in 10^{17} in picking the one with the 'x' on it" (MacArthur, *How To Study the Bible*, p. 17).

B. Christ

Christ Himself did not waver on the authority of Scripture (Matthew 5:18). He used it to defeat Satan (Matthew 4:1-11) and appealed to it as the record of salvation (John 5:39).

C. Miracles

The purpose of the witness of miracles was to attest to the truth of the message connected to it.

1. Exodus 4:28-31
2. Matthew 9:5,6
3. John 5:36
4. Acts 2:22
5. Hebrews 2:4

These were testimonies to the truths the apostles and Christ were teaching.

D. Experience

While certainly not the most authoritative proof, experience does bear witness of the authenticity of the Word of God. Second Corinthians 5:17 declares that when one receives Christ, he/she is a "new creation". Testimony upon testimony of life-change can be attributed to a proper response to the message of the Book!

III. AIM OF THE BIBLE

  A. It provides us with d*octrinal* truth.

     1. God

     2. Christ

     3. Holy Spirit

     4. Man

     5. Angels

     6. Salvation

     7. Sin

     8. Future

  B. It provides us with p*ractical* truth.

     1. Guidelines concerning temptation

     2. Guidelines concerning trials

     3. Guidelines concerning marriage

     4. Guidelines concerning children

     5. Guidelines concerning finances

     6. Guidelines concerning lifestyle

     7. Guidelines concerning problems

     8. Guidelines concerning work

     9. Guidelines concerning church

Understanding the attributes of the Bible, the authenticity of the Bible, and the aim of the Bible, we should be all the more motivated toward diligent study so that we may truly be the ministers of truth that God wants us to be.

IV. Outline of Books of the Bible

BOOK	DIVISION	
	MINOR	MAJOR
Genesis	Pentateuch	The Law
Exodus		
Leviticus		
Numbers		
Deuteronomy		
Joshua	Historical	Writings
Judges		
Ruth		
First Samuel		
Second Samuel		
First Kings		
Second Kings		
First Chronicles		
Second Chronicles		
Ezra		
Nehemiah		
Esther		
Job	Poetical	
Psalms		
Proverbs		
Ecclesiastes		
Song of Solomon		
Isaiah	Major Prophets	Prophets
Jeremiah		
Lamentations		
Ezekiel		
Daniel		
Hosea	Minor Prophets	
Joel		
Amos		
Obadiah		
Jonah		
Micah		
Nahum		
Habakkuk		
Zephaniah		
Haggai		
Zechariah		
Malachi		

BOOK	DIVISION	
	MINOR	MAJOR
Matthew	Gospels	Historical
Mark		
Luke		
John		
Acts	Acts of the Apostles	
Romans	Epistles of Paul	Epistles
First Corinthians		
Second Corinthians		
Galatians		
Ephesians		
Philippians		
Colossians		
First Thessalonians		
Second Thessalonians		
First Timothy		
Second Timothy		
Titus		
Philemon		
Hebrews	Epistle to the Hebrews	
James	Epistle of James	
First Peter	Epistles of Peter	
Second Peter		
First John	Epistles of John	
Second John		
Third John		
Jude	Epistle of Jude	
Revelation	Revelation	Apocalypse

SECTION 2

Tools for Bible Study

As in digging for buried treasure, the better the tools, the more efficient the dig. Below are some guidelines for effective tools for the study of God's treasure.

I. BIBLES

    A. Translations of the Bible

    Translations of the Bible fall into three primary categories:

    1) Literal – word-for-word translation

    2) Free – thought-by-thought translation or sentence-by-sentence

    3) Paraphrase – a paraphrase of the text

    While this is not an exhaustive study on the families of translations, we will examine the benefits and weaknesses of each of the major translations. In the English language there are five translations used by churches and Christians. We will focus on the history of these texts, their strengths and their weaknesses.

    1. THE KING JAMES VERSION (KJV)

    Also known as the Authorized Version (AV)

        a. History

        Because of the variety of independent versions, the Puritans petitioned King James 1 in 1603. This resulted in a conference at Hampton Court in 1604, from which the following is an excerpt:

> "That a translation be made of the whole Bible, as consonant as can be to the original Hebrew and Greek; and this to be set out and printed, without any marginal notes, and only to be used in all churches of England in time of divine service."

        Work began in 1607, and the version was complete in 1611. Fifty men made up six panels of translators. Three panels worked on the Old Testament, two panels on the New Testament, and one panel on the Apocrypha.

        In 1611, three revisions were accomplished. The first was known as the "He" Bible, and the last two called the "She" Bible, because of their respective renderings of Ruth 3:15.

The revision made at Cambridge in 1762 and at Oxford in 1769 modernized the language of the previous Authorized Versions. These are the revisions that make up our King James Version.

b. Features

A very literal and reliable translation, based upon the Byzantine family of manuscripts and the Majority Text. Its major drawback is the use of archaic and obsolete words which make its reading difficult at times for the modern reader.

2. THE REVISED STANDARD VERSION (RSV)

   a. History

   "The Revised Standard Version of the Bible is an authorized revision of the American Standard Version, published in 1901, which was a revision of the King James Version, published in 1611" (Preface, p.iii).

   b. Features

   This text has often come into question for its consistent bent toward liberal theology in what text they choose. Some examples are Colossians 1:14, Acts 8:37, and Isaiah 7:14. The RSV is basically a literal translation, though often not used by conservative evangelicals because of their concerns over these liberal tendencies.

3. NEW AMERICAN STANDARD BIBLE (NASB)

   a. History

   This translation was realized because of the perceived need to incorporate recent textual discoveries as well as rendering it into more modern English (than the 1901 American Standard Version). The editorial team completed this version in 1971.

   b. Features

   "When it was felt that the word-for-word literalness was unacceptable to the modern reader, a change was made in the direction of a more current English idiom" (Preface). While it is idiomatic, it still may be considered a literal translation. The NASB is based primarily on the New Testament work of the *Nestle's Novum Testamentum Text* (based on the Alexandrian family of manuscripts).

Because of its exclusive reliance on the fewer and older manuscripts, it often omits or notes omissions in its margin of various texts (i.e., Colossians 1:14).

4. THE NEW INTERNATIONAL VERSION (NIV)

   a. History

   This version was developed by establishing a series of three committees:

   1. The translation by the translators of the books of the Bible provides a basis.

   2. These translations were then reviewed by one of the Intermediate Editorial Committees for revision. From that point it went to the General Editorial Committee, who would make further revisions.

   3. The Committee on Bible Translation was the final revision. The actual work of the NIV was completed in 1978.

   b. Features

   While proclaiming to work from all families of the Greek text, the desire for a modern English translation resulted in the NIV being a free rather than a very literal translation.

   It eliminates a large amount of verses from the actual text (Matthew 17:21; Matthew 18:11; Matthew 23:14; Mark 7:16; Mark 9:44; Mark 9:46; Mark 11:26; Mark 15:28; Luke 17:36;; Luke 23:17; John 5:3-4; Acts 8:37; Acts 15:34; Acts 24:7; Acts 28:29; Romans 16:24). This does not include a number of *portions* from the other verses. Some of its translations are weak (1 Timothy 3:16 "he" instead of "God").

   As a translation, it too often interprets (i.e. 1 Samuel 15:33 "and Samuel put Agag to death"; 1 Peter 1:2 "for obedience to Jesus Christ").

   This translation may be helpful in Bible Study, but must be recognized as a free translation and not a literal translation.

5. THE NEW KING JAMES VERSION (NKJV)

   a. History

   The Preface of the 1611 AV stated that the purpose was not "to make a new translation…but to make a good one better." They spoke of the Bishops Bible. The New King James editors used this purpose to refer to their new translation.

In the Old Testament, the translators drew from a number of ancient Hebrew texts, the Septuagint, the Vulgate, and relevant portions from the Dead Sea Scrolls.

The New Testament was based upon the Byzantine texts, with references made to various manuscripts discovered since the Authorized Version was completed. This work was completed in 1982.

b. Features

The NKJV includes variant readings in the Margin of the U (Nestle's Greek) and the M (Majority Text) should there be differences in the manuscript witness.

It also includes the fullness of the King James Version and the literal translating which characterized the KJV.

Finally, this translation eliminates the archaic or obsolete words and replaces them with accurately translated alternatives.

6. The English Standard Version (ESV)

a. History

The ESV has grown out of the Tyndale and King James legacy. The 1971 RSV text was its starting point. The ESV had a 14-member Translation Oversight Committee that benefited from the work of 50 biblical experts.

The translators drew mostly from the Masoretic Text for much of the Hebrew. In some cases, they looked to the Dead Sea Scrolls, the Septuagint, the Samaritan Pentateuch, and other sources.

The Greek text was based mostly on the 1993 editions of the *Greek New Testament* (4th corrected ed.) published by United Bible Societies (UBS) and the *Novum Testamentum Graece* (27th ed.) edited by Nestle and Aland. The translators used other Greek manuscripts to help with difficult passages, but only sparingly.

b. Features

The ESV is an "essentially literal" translation and seeks to be transparent to the original text. Like the NKJV, it updates the archaic or obsolete wording of the KJV for a more accurate understanding. Like the KJV, there are language study tools for a word-for-word rendering of the original words.

B. Study Bibles

There are a number of Study Bibles available today. Here are just a few of them.

1. *The MacArthur Study Bible*

    a. This in-text study is excellent as a reference.

    b. The introduction for each book provides the reader with information about the historical background (title and authorship) as well as an overview of its contents.

    c. Key information under the text aids readers in understanding the text.

    d. Introduction to the Bible

    e. How We Got the Bible

    f. How to Study the Bible

    g. Topical Index

    h. Overview of Theology

2. *ESV Study Bible*

    a. Like *The MacArthur Study Bible*, this has excellent in-text reference notes and introductions to each book.

    b. Over 200 full-color maps, created with the latest satellite imagery

    c. More than 40 illustrations

    d. Over 200 excellent charts offering key insights and analysis

3. *Thompson Chain Reference Bible*

    a. A number system on the side margin allows a person to study a text topically.

    b. In the back are eight departments to which this numbering system is linked:

        1) Text-cyclopedia

2) Outline Studies

3) Analysis of Bible Books

4) Character Studies

5) Harmonies and Illustrated Studies

6) Archaeological Supplement

7) Concordance

8) Indexed Atlas

4. *Ryrie Study Bible*

   a. This is another excellent reference for in-text study.

   b. The introduction for each book provides the reader with information about the historical background (title and authorship) as well as an overview of its contents.

   c. Again, key information under the text helps readers to understand the text.

   d. The back provides a number of helps:

      1) Harmony of the Gospels

      2) Survey of Bible Doctrines

      3) Background and History of the Bible

      4) Helpful Tables of Information

      5) Topical Index

      6) Concordance

      7) Maps

5. *New Open Bible*

   a. Nelson's publishers released this version.

   b. The *New Open Bible* offers several supplemental features.

      1) Concise book introductions

      2) Cross-references

      3) 40 in-depth word studies

      4) 48 in-text maps

      5) 100 illustrated Bible close-ups

6) Includes a "How to Study the Bible" section

6. Other Study Bibles

   a. *Comparative Study Bible*

   b. *Reese Chronological Bible*

   c. *Cults Reference Bible*

II. CONCORDANCES

A. The Objective

A concordance gives the lay-person an opportunity to glean from the original languages of the Bible while not having to know a thing about them.

This reference tool is used by first looking up the word in the English as it appears in the text. The number corresponds with an entry in the back that provides an explanation of the word.

B. Suggested Options

1. *Strong's Exhaustive Concordance*

2. *Cruden's Concordance*

3. *Young's Analytical Concordance*

III. BIBLE HANDBOOK

A. Their Objective

Bible handbooks provide the opportunity to understand an overview of any book, glean valuable background information, and see the overview of even the content of a book.

B. Suggested Options

1. *Unger's Bible Handbook*

2. *Halley's Bible Handbook*

3. *The Baker Bible Handbook*

4. *Walk Thru the Bible*

IV. DICTIONARIES

There are a variety of tools that bear the title "dictionary." In order to eliminate any confusion, we will consider three types of dictionaries.

A. Expository Dictionaries

1. The Objective

   Probably the most similar to common English dictionaries, expository dictionaries offer similar information regarding word definitions in the original languages of Scripture passages.

2. Suggested Options

   a. *Vine's Expository Dictionary* (New Testament)

   b. *Nelson's Expository Dictionary* (Old Testament)

   c. *Theological Wordbook of the Old Testament*

B. Bible Dictionaries

1. The Objective

   Bible dictionaries furnish the student of God's Word with background information on various people, places, and things of the Bible.

2. Suggested Options

   a. *Unger's Bible Dictionary*

   b. *Nelson's Illustrated Bible Dictionary*

   c. *New Bible Dictionary*

C. Theological Dictionaries

1. The Objective

   This type of dictionary supplies background information on various theologies, their history, and those who held them. These also supply biographies on key leaders in church history.

2. Suggested Options

   a. *Evangelical* Dictionary of Theology (Elwell)

   b. *New Dictionary of Theology* (Ferguson, etc.)

School of Biblical Hermeneutics   Page 16

V. OTHER HELPFUL TOOLS

   A. Bible Commentaries

      1. The Objective

         Commentaries provide the student with insight from those who have studied the entire content.

         WARNING: Before you use a commentary, it is important that you know the background of its author. The way a person interprets certain things may be influenced by his or her theological background.

      2. Suggested Options (on the whole Bible)

         a. *Jamison-Fausset-Brown Commentary*

         b. *Expositor's Bible Commentary*

         c. *Bible Knowledge Commentary*

         d. *Everyman's Bible Commentary*

         e. *Tyndale Bible Commentary*

   B. Bible Geography

      1. Their Objective

         These tools for study provide maps which correspond to certain Bible events, geographic descriptions, as well as archaeological information.

      2. Suggested Options

         a. *MacMillan Bible Atlas*

         b. *Moody Atlas of the Bible*

   C. Bible Encyclopedias

      1. The Objective

         These are expanded Bible dictionaries, typically printed in more than one volume.

      2. Suggested Options

         a. *International Standard Bible Encyclopedia (ISBE)*

b. *Zondervan Pictorial Bible Encyclopedia*

D. Books on Customs and Manners

1. The Objective

    Customs and Manners books provide topical studies typically on the home, money, trade, schooling, etc. during Bible times. Note that much of this information may also be found in Bible dictionaries or encyclopedias.

2. Suggested Options

    a. *Handbook of Life in Bible Times* (*Thompson*)

    b. *Today's Handbook of Bible Times and Customs* (*Coleman*)

VI. Computer Software

A. Logos

1. Books, books, and more books

    Logos has more books available than any other software package and provides the widest range of material.

2. Searching

    The searching ability makes Logos worth its price. It allows the user to sift through thousands of books within minutes. Additionally, Logos provides many different ways to search through its library so that the results can be tailored to reflect a specific idea.

3. Integrated Tools

    Logos provides a well-integrated tool set great for personal Bible study or serious research. The integration makes it easy to access original language help.

B. Bible Works

    The strength of this tool is its original language research. It has one of the best Greek works. Serious Bible students will find Bible Works more useful than will casual Bible students.

C. Ages

    Ages provides inexpensive books in an Adobe PDF format. Adobe does not, however, provide much in the way of search tools or integrated books.

VII. Websites

Note: The mentioning of these websites is not an endorsement. Discernment is always required, especially on the internet.

http://bible.crosswalk.com – Commentaries and Bible passage search online

http://biblos.com – A complete Bible study site that has everything necessary for study at one location

http://www.virtualseminary.net – Many books online

http://www.biblebb.com – Many online sermons, including John MacArthur

http://www.iclnet.org – Mega-site of books

http://www.ccel.org – Mega-site of classic Christian literature

http://www.puritansermons.com – Mega-site of Puritan sermons and books

http://www.sermoncentral.com – A site full of sermons

http://executableoutlines.com – Outlines and overview of Bible books

http://www.bible.org – Home of the NET Bible and many other resources

http://www.answersingenesis.org – Many creation science articles

http://www.creationontheweb.com/ - More creation science articles

http://www.carm.org – Christian apologetics and research materials

http://www.str.org – More Christian apologetic materials

SECTION 3

Keys to Biblical Hermeneutics: Inductive Bible Study

Inductive Bible study is the process of allowing the Scriptures to interpret themselves. Moving from the big picture to the details allows interpretation to be determined by context. We need to identify the incorrect methods of interpretation and the correct model of interpretation.

I. Models of Interpretation

   A. Incorrect Models of Interpretation

   Among those who respect the authority and validity of the Bible, there are basically three false methods of interpretations.

   1. Isolationism – Interpreting a verse or passage without regard for the context in which it is found.

   2. Proof texting – Stringing a series of verses together often interpreted apart from their context (isolationism), in order to prove or develop a certain theology.

   3. Spiritualizing – Reading a truth (either spiritually or historically) into a text or book of the Bible.

   B. Correct Model of Interpretation

   We believe in the literal-normal model of interpretation which embraces the following truths:

   1. Scripture is to be interpreted in its historical context.

   2. Scripture is to be interpreted according to the normal rules of grammar (including the recognition of literary devices).

   3. Scripture is to be interpreted according to its context.

There are four keys to understanding God's Word using an inductive Bible study: identification, investigation, interpretation, and implementation.

KEY # 1: IDENTIFICATION

In order to interpret correctly any passage, students of Scripture must first recognize what type of literature they are investigating. There are basically five types of literature represented in Scripture: historical narrative, poetry, wisdom literature, prophetic revelation, and epistles of instruction. Each of these types of literature has different rules of interpretation.

I. Historical Narrative

   A. Books of the Bible which are historical narratives:

      1. Old Testament

         Genesis-Ruth

         1 and 2 Samuel

         1 and 2 Kings

         1 and 2 Chronicles

         Ezra

         Nehemiah

         Esther

      2. New Testament

         Matthew

         Mark

         Luke

         John

         Acts

   B. Keys to interpreting historical literature

      1. Narratives do not directly teach doctrine.

      2. Narratives do not always record what should happen. They simply record what happened.

      3. Narratives do not always include a statement as to whether the event was good or bad.

4. Narratives are not allegories with hidden meanings.

5. Narratives are stories about God first.

II. Poetic Literature

   A. Books of the Bible which are poetic literature

   Psalms

   Song of Solomon

   Plus portions of many Old Testament Books

   B. Keys to interpreting poetic literature

   Hebrew poetry includes the following types of parallelism:

   1. *Synonymous* parallelism (Psalm 3:1)

      The second line says the same thing as the first for emphasis.

   2. *Synthetic* parallelism (Psalm 95:3)

      The second line builds up the thought of the first.

   3. *Emblematic* parallelism (Psalm 42:1)

      The first line illustrates the content of the second.

   4. *Antithetical* parallelism (Psalm 1:6)

      The first line is coupled with the second to form a contrast.

   5. *Climatic* parallelism (Psalm 29:1)

      The second line completes the first by repeating part of the first and then expanding.

   6. *Formal* parallelism (Psalm 2:6)

      Two lines together express a thought or theme.

III. Wisdom Literature

   A. Books of the Bible which are wisdom literature

   Job

   Proverbs

   Ecclesiastes

   B. Keys to interpreting wisdom literature

   1. Wisdom literature is advice from those who had learned valuable life lessons.

   2. Wisdom literature uses maxims, short statements of truth.

   3. Wisdom literature uses a variety of literary devices.

      a. Parallelism (see above)

      b. Comparison (Proverbs 22:1)

      c. Contrasts (Proverbs 10:1-14)

      d. Metaphors and Similes (Proverbs 26:23)

      e. Portraits (Proverbs 31:1-=31)

      f. Vignettes (Proverbs 27:23-27)

IV. Prophetic Literature

   A. Books of the Bible which are prophetic

      Isaiah

      Jeremiah

      Lamentations

      Ezekiel

      Daniel

      Hosea

      Joel

      Amos

      Obadiah

      Jonah

      Micah

      Nahum

      Habakkuk

      Zephaniah

      Haggai

      Zechariah

      Malachi

      Revelation

   B. Keys to interpreting prophetic literature

      In order to understand prophetic literature, these issues need to be addressed carefully:

      1. Identity of the prophet

      2. The reason why the prophet spoke

      3. His audience

      4. The time of his prophecies

V. Instruction from the Epistles

   A. Books of the Bible which are epistles (letters)

      Romans

      1 Corinthians

      2 Corinthians

      Galatians

      Ephesians

      Philippians

      Colossians

      1 Thessalonians

      2 Thessalonians

      1 Timothy

      2 Timothy

      Titus

      Philemon

      Hebrews

      James

      1 Peter

      2 Peter

      1 John

      2 John

      3 John

      Jude

   B. Keys to interpreting epistles

      New Testament epistles are very special and vital for our faith for a number of reasons:

      1. Epistles are letters of instruction for the churches.

      2. They were written by their authors to a specific group which had specific problems or needs.

KEY # 2: INVESTIGATION

Read through the text you are studying a number of times from two or more versions if possible. As you read through the text, write down the answers to these significant questions:

I. What?

Identify key themes, events, and any key indicators of the structure of the text. Look for recurring words (e.g. "ungodly" in Jude), phrases (e.g. "God forbid" [KJV] in Romans), and addresses to specific groups (e.g. wives, husbands, children, etc., in Ephesians). Note Old Testament quotations in the New Testament.

II. Who?

Determine who the writer, the recipient(s), or any other characters mentioned in the text are. Note any comments about these people (nationality, occupation, family, character, or any other significant features).

III. Why?

Look for the reason(s) why the author wrote what he wrote. This is the purpose of the book. Sometimes it is found in one verse (e.g. John 20:31; 1 John 5:13) or repetitious themes (e.g. "suffering" in 1 Peter and "these are the generations of" in Genesis). Some books have more than one purpose (e.g. Hebrews seeming to have both a Christian and non-Christian audience).

IV. When?

Observe any indicators of time in the book regarding when it was written. Pay attention to times of day, the mentioning of months or years, and any feasts or holidays connected to the text. These unlock insight into the book (e.g. Nehemiah 1:1; 2:1). It is also important to note where the book fits into the plan of the church or the plan of Israel.

V. Where?

Are there any significant geographical features? Are there mentions of locality in the text (i.e. cities, types of geography, seas, rivers, countries, etc.)?

KEY # 3: INTERPRETATION

Once we have written our first impressions and general observations of the text, we will begin employing some of our tools.

I. Charting the Passage

   A. Determine the units of thought.

      1. Divide the passage into paragraphs.

         These are usually identified by bold verse numbers, paragraph marks, or headings.

      2. In the New Testament epistles (Romans-Jude), it is beneficial to identify the sentences within each paragraph. Since these books of the Bible are instructional in nature, the sentences will provide support for the themes of each paragraph. This is not necessary in historical books, prophetic books, or in poetry.

         There are also recorded sermons for which this may be a beneficial approach (e.g. Acts 2:14-36).

   B. Determine their link with the preceding and proceeding passage.

      What do the preceding and succeeding paragraphs of information have to do with the context?

II. Examining the Context

   A. Background to the characters

      1. Within the book

      2. In other books of the Bible

      3. In outside sources

   B. Key themes and events

      1. Observe comments in a Study Bible or dictionary.

      2. Write definitions of key words as they fit into the context.

   C. Time factor

      1. Find out the date of book.

School of Biblical Hermeneutics   Page 31

      2. Observe any other books of the Bible that may give you insight into the historical setting.

      3. Look up historical information which will give you insight into the historical setting, the feasts, etc.

  D. The purpose(s) or reason(s)

      1. What is the need of the recipient?

      2. What is the message of the writer?

  E. The location and geography

      1. Note the place of the recipients, and study the events in that place at that time.

      2. Look up information on cities, countries, bodies of water, etc. that are relevant to understanding the text.

III. Comparing the Scriptures

Using a Topical Bible, a topical index in a Study Bible, or a cross-reference apparatus, compare your information to other Scriptures related to the themes of the passage.

IV. Consulting Another Student

This is where referencing a commentary would enhance one's understanding of the text by placing some of the details into the flow of the text.

V. Synthesizing Your Study

KEY # 4: IMPLEMENTATION

First Corinthians 8:1 warns that "knowledge puffs up, but love edifies." James encouraged his readers to "be doers of the word and not hearers only." These passages remind us that the goal of studying the Scriptures is NOT simply for knowledge, but to CHANGE OUR LIVES!!

I. Evaluating Your Strengths and Weaknesses

   This is where true life changes happen. We need to examine ourselves honestly and identify our aptitudes and vulnerabilities.

II. Applying Your Study to Your Life

   A. Social

   B. Family

   C. Church

   D. Work

   E. Relationship with God

   F. Personal

   G. Emotional

   H. Finances

   I. Physical

   J. Thoughts

   K. Recreation and time

II. Determining the Principles for Life from Your Study

III. Being Honest and Humble to Your Findings

IV. Meditating on the Truths

V. Writing or Memorizing Key Verses or Principles

SECTION 4

Alternative Types of Study

This section will provide the student with two different avenues by which one may study the Scriptures. An important truth needs to be emphasized concerning any type of study: any study must be based on a correct interpretation of the Scripture.

We will introduce biographical studies, topical, and analytical studies.

I. Biographical Bible Studies

    A. Choose a Bible character to study.

    B. Locate all the revelation on that particular character.

        This can be done by means of cross-referencing and concordances.

        EXAMPLE: For the life of Abraham, we see references not only in the book of Genesis but throughout the Old Testament and the New Testament. Here is a list of the books in which Abraham is mentioned: Exodus, Leviticus, Numbers, Psalms, Isaiah, Jeremiah, Ezekiel, Micah, Matthew, Mark, Luke, John, Acts, Romans, 2 Corinthians, Galatians, Hebrews, James, and 1 Peter (20 books total).

    C. Look for these features:

        1. Dates

            Bible studies or dictionaries may help you in this area. Also notice references of time when dealing with biographies (i.e. mentioning of months and years of reign, feasts, holidays, etc).

            Try to appreciate the historical setting that the character you are studying is experiencing.

        2. Family

            a. Parents

            b. Wife

            c. Children

            d. Other Family

For example, for the life of Abraham, we see that his father was Terah, his wife Sarah, his children were Isaac and Ishmael (plus others), and his nephew was Lot.

Notice carefully the positive and negative interactions in these relationships.

D. Conversion

Note the circumstances and the results. These, however, are not often mentioned in the Scriptures.

E. Ministry/Vocation

Notice the type of ministry or lack of ministry your character has. Note the positive and negative aspects of ministering to others.

F. Death

Note the causes or any significant features surrounding the character's death.

G. Key Verses

These are any significant verses that would be practical for your life.

H. Points to Practice

Notice any virtues of the character you are studying. Taking David as an example, you will note characteristics such as courage, submission to government, steadfastness in trials, etc.

I. Points to Shun

Taking the same example, notice various vices such as adultery, murder, etc.

J. Life Illustrations

Point out what truths your character best illustrates in life. Some examples:

1. Abraham – Faith that works

2. Solomon – Knowing more than you do

3. Paul – Zeal for evangelism

4. Peter – Zeal which had to be learned

K. Relevant Outside Resources

There are various books that may give you further insight on the character you are studying.

II. Doctrinal (Topical) Bible Studies

A. Define the boundaries of your study.

1. Topic

The topic may be as general (a topical study of Christ) or as specific (a topical study of Christ's method of witnessing) as desired.

Remember, though, that the broader the topic, the greater the revelation to be handled.

2. Text

You may want to limit your study to a certain part of the Bible. For example, instead of doing a study on the Holy Spirit in the Bible, you may want to do a study on the Holy Spirit in the Old Testament, the Holy Spirit in the gospels, etc.

B. Organize the information.

1. Chronologically

Here are some examples:

a. Life of Christ

b. Eschatology

c. Development of the church

2. Development in Scripture

Organize material as it appeared in Scripture by placing the information as it fits into these categories:

a. Old Testament

b. Gospels

c. New Testament

d. End Times

This type of organization would be beneficial for studies like the ministry of the Holy Spirit or the means for the presentation of the Gospel.

3. Subtopics

   Taking the topical study and breaking it down into related themes is another approach.

4. Synthesis of the Organization

   CHRONOLOGICAL STUDY OF THE LIFE OF CHRIST

   a. The Early Life of Christ

      i. His birth

      ii. His childhood

   b. The Ministry of Christ

      i. His public ministry

      ii. His private ministry

   c. The Death of Christ

      i. The betrayal

      ii. The trial

      iii. The crucifixion

      iv. The resurrection

      v. The ascension

   DEVELOPMENTAL STUDY OF THE LIFE OF CHRIST

a. Christ in the Old Testament

      i. Prophecy

      ii. Personal

   b. Christ in the Gospels and Acts

   c. Christ in the Epistles

   d. Christ in Revelation

   SUBTOPICAL STUDY OF THE LIFE OF CHRIST

   a. The Prayer life of Christ

      i. Methods

      ii. Content

   b. The Evangelism of Christ

      i. Methods

      ii. Message

   c. The Discipling of Christ

      i. Teaching techniques

      iii. Modeling

   d. Christ's Way of Dealing with Temptation

   e. Christ's Way of Dealing with Trials

III. Analytical Bible Study

The analytical method of Bible study is taking the whole apart into smaller sections for thorough analyzing.

It must be remembered that this type of Bible study is built on the principles of inductive study. Using this kind of study in the epistles is effective.

   A. Choose a text.

   The key with the analytical method of Bible study is to avoid tackling too many passages at once.

B. Break down the passage with a block diagram.

1. Keep main thoughts and clauses to the left of the vertical chart.

2. Indent subordinate clauses.

3. Note the punctuation in English Bibles. While these were never inspired, they are mostly accurate gauges to determine main points and sub-points.

4. Notice subordinate words that explain nouns and verbs.

   EXAMPLES: Nouns = who, whom, which, etc.

   Verbs = that, so that, because, words ending in "ing"

   From here the process of investigation is similar to what we have seen before, but the detail may be much deeper.

We can spend a lifetime studying the Bible and still not exhaust its depths and riches. Hopefully, this study will set a foundation for the proper interpretation of the Word of God to understand the Scriptures rightly.

BIBLIOGRAPHY

Barber, Cyril. J. *Dynamic Personal Bible Study.* Neptune, New Jersey: Loizeaux Brothers, 1981

Braga, James. *How to Study the Bible.* Portland, Oregon: Multnomah Press, 1982.

Finzel, Hans. *Opening the Book.* Wheaton, Illinois: Victor Books. 1987.

Jensen, Irving L. *Independent Bible Study.* Chicago, Illinois: Moody Press, 1963.

MacArthur, John. *How to Study the Bible.* Chicago, Illinois: Moody Press, 1982.

Vos, Howard F. *Effective Bible Study.* Grand Rapids, Michigan: Zondervan Publishing House, 1956.

All Scripture quotations, unless otherwise noted, are from the New King James Version, Thomas Nelson, Inc., 1982.